AUSTRALIA

The Ultimate Australia Travel Guide By A Traveler For A Traveler

The Best Travel Tips: Where To Go, What To See And Much More

SECOND EDITION

Why Lost Travelers Guides?

First, we want to wish you an amazing time in Australia when you plan to visit. Also we would like to thank you and congratulate you for downloading our travel guide, *"Australia; The Ultimate Australia Travel Guide By A Traveler For A Traveler"*.

Allow us to explain our beginnings, and the reason we created Lost Travelers. Lost Travelers was created due to one simple problem that other guides on the market did not solve; loss of time. Considering it's the 21ˢᵗ century and everything is available on the internet why do we still purchase guidebooks? To save us time! That's right.

Since the goal is to be efficient and save time, we did not understand why there are several guidebooks on the market that are of 500 to 1000 page' long. We do not believe one needs that much bluff to get an overview of the location and some remarkable suggestions. Considering many guidebooks on the market are filled with "suggestions" that were sponsored for, we have decided to take a different approach and provide our travelers with an honest opinion and decline any sort of sponsorship. This simply allows us to cut off any nonsense and create our guides the Lost Travelers style.

Our mission is simple; to create an easy to follow guide book that outlines the best of activities to do in our limited time at the destination. This easily saves you your most valuable asset; your time. You no longer need to spend hours looking through a massive book, or spend hours searching for information on the internet as we have completed the whole process for you. The best part is we provide you our e-guides for one third the price of the leading brand, and our paper copy for only half the price.

Thanks again for choosing us, we hope you enjoy!

Table Of Contents

AUSTRALIA

Bojangles Saloon &
Restaurant Alice Springs

Taronga Zoo

Blue Mountains

Airport Link

Cruise Ships dock at the
overseas Passenger Terminal

Sydney Visitor Center at the
Rocks

Wynard City Rail Station

Watsons Bay -

Sydney Pass

Captain Cook's Coffee Cruise
Sunset walk on Sydney Harbour
bully
Sydney Opera house tour
Sydney Tower
Macquarie St - Sydney Colonial
Histy Sydney most elegant Blvd.

Sydney Harbor Nat Park
Garden Island   Manley Beach

Observatory Hill (Windmill Hill)
St James Church. Lunchtime concerts
on Wednesdays.
Australian National Maritime Museum
Sydney Aquarium   Sydney Tower
Marble Bar   Koala Park
Queen Victoria Building Sanctuary
    St Andrews Cathedral The Rocks
                          Market

Chapter 1: A Brief History of Australia

Australia's history is steeped with a mixture of Aboriginal and British colonial influences. To this day, this mixture is apparent in many aspects of modern Australian culture and lifestyle

The Aborigines

The Australian archipelago has been occupied by natives known as the Aborigines for almost 80,000 years. Experts believe that there were at least 300 different Aboriginal tribes scattered around the mainland, as well as in the surrounding little islands including the island of Tasmania. Each of these tribes had its own cultures and traditions, though there were many similarities between them especially in terms of their relationship with the environment. It is also believed that Australia's Aborigines are related to the native inhabitants of many Southeast Asian nations.

After travelling from Southeast Asia by boat, the Aboriginal tribes settled down in various locales around Australia. Most of the Aborigines settled in regions that were closest to the sea and other water form like rivers and lakes. They mostly lived a nomadic lifestyle, never settling down in one specific place for a long period of time. Their migration patterns were mostly dependent on maximizing the availability of food in a certain area.

By moving away from a specific hunting ground for about a year or for one season, the Aborigines gave that area sufficient time to regenerate. This lack of permanent dwelling was probably one of the reasons why the early European explorers who came in the 1600's assumed that Australia was an uninhabited land.

The Europeans

Contrary to popular belief, the English were not the first Europeans to set foot in Australian soil. The Dutch have already discovered the land in 1606. However, they were not interested in colonizing it as they deemed it uninhabitable. Instead, they focused their efforts in the countries around Asia that became known as the Indies.

The British came in 1770 on an exploration led by Captain James Cook. His instructions were specific: to colonize the land regardless if it was inhabited or not. In the event that there were any inhabitants, he was supposed to seek their permission first prior to creating a settlement. Permission was not sought from the natives since Cook deemed the land uninhabited. This assumption was based on the fact that none of the dwellings looked permanent or fenced in.

However, it wasn't until 1788 when the first British settlers arrived and a formal British colony was established. The initial settlers consisted of up to 1,500 people that were transported in a fleet of 11 ships. Almost half of these initial settlers were convicts from the overflowing jails in England. These first settlers arrived in Sydney Cove and the settlement of New South Wales (NSW) was the very first town to be established. Between 1770 and 1840, a total number of 160,000 convicts were settled in New South Wales.

After the settlement in Sydney was established, two other settlements followed. The second British colony was established in 1804 in the island of Tasmania, which was then called Van Diemen's Land. The third was in South Australia (SA) in 1836 although convicts were never transported there. Transportation of convicts to Tasmania stopped in 1825. Another territory was later established in Western Australia but this was done by immigrants who came of their own volition.

The Next Wave of Migrants

It should first be noted that even in popular context, the first wave of migrants from Britain are sometimes referred to as squatters. This is because they settled in lands that originally belonged to the Aborigines. In most instances, land settlement was often accompanied by bloodshed and the decimation of most of the Aboriginal population. However, the biggest threat to the Aborigines was not the migrant's guns but the diseases that they brought with them.

As early as the 1790's, free settlers have already started coming to Australia in waves. More of them arrived in the 1850's during the gold rush in NSW and Victoria (VIC). This time, it wasn't just people who wanted to settle in a new land that arrived. They weren't all British nationals as well. The new wave also brought with it people from other countries, specifically traders and entertainers.

The wave of migration to Australia hasn't stopped even to this day. As of January 2015, the estimated number of migrants was around 6.6 million. This number contributes to at least 50% of the country's population growth. These migrants came from over 200 countries in Asia and in other parts of the world. Subsequently, these migrants have brought major aspects of their home country's culture over to their new place of residence. This then contributes to the eclectic mix of cultures that characterizes modern-day Australia.

Chapter 2: Australia's Geography and Climate

Geography

Australia is both a country and a continent. It is also an archipelago that encompasses at least 7.6 square kilometers of land. It is consisting of two main masses of land:

- Mainland Australia
- Tasmania

Australia is bounded on all sides by the sea. As a matter of fact, it is surrounded by the Pacific Ocean that lies at its Eastern point and the Indian Ocean on its western point. Several seas separate the country from its nearest neighbors, including:

- The Timor Sea – this lies along Australia's northwestern coast and separates it from Indonesia.
- The Arafura Sea – this lies along the northernmost tip and separates the country from Papua New Guinea, which is its closest neighbor.
- The Tasman Sea – this lies along the southeastern coast and separates the country from New Zealand.

Australia is also one of the oldest landmasses in the world. This means that most of its landscape has gone through long-term erosion. This is why the country mostly consists of wide expanses of flat arid desert land specifically along its central regions. It also means that most of the country's soil is quite old and is no longer fertile. Some of its rock formations also date back to millions of years ago.

However, thanks to its size, the country also consists of a variety of other land forms including:

- Tropical rainforest mostly along the northeastern portion.

- Mountain ranges along the southern and eastern portions including Tasmania.

The country's size also means that the climate could vary depending on the location.

Climate

Australia is consists of 5 different climate zones, including:

1. Equatorial zone (Tropical Savannah climate) – this climate mostly affects the northernmost tips of the archipelago. This includes the tips of the Northern Territory (NT) and a small portion of the city of Darwin. Cape York on the northern tip of Queensland (QLD) also has a tropical savannah climate. This means that these areas get at least 6 months of the dry season and at least another 6 months of the wet season.

2. Tropical zone (Tropical Monsoon climate) – this climate affects the upper half of the Northern Territory from the coast along the Joseph Bonaparte Gulf to the areas north of the Roper River. In QLD, this climate is felt along the entire Cape York Peninsula and along the eastern coast of Cairns down to Townsville. It also affects the Kimberley region of Western Australia (WA). The duration of the wet and the dry seasons are also

relatively equal, although these areas receive a higher volume of monsoon rains.

3. Subtropical zone – this consists mostly of the eastern half of QLD up to the inner part of Cairns. It also includes a small area on the northern part of NSW, as well as its northeastern coast. A small portion of WA starting from Perth down to Geraldton also belongs to this zone. These areas experience a longer duration of the dry, sunny weather. The climate here is often likened to the climate in the Mediterranean countries. The cold season mostly consists of mild rainfall.

4. Desert zone (Arid or Semi-arid climate) – the desert climate affects a large portion of WA specifically the central areas of mainland Australia. It also includes the surrounding areas around the lower half of NT, about 80% of the land area of SA, and a small portion QLD along its far southwestern region starting from Mt Isa to Thargomindah. The northwestern portion of NSW is also affected. These regions form part of Australia's five major deserts, specifically:

    a. The Great Sandy Desert
    b. Gibson Desert
    c. Great Victorian Desert
    d. Tanami Desert
    e. Simpson Desert

Grasslands or savannahs surround the desert areas. It comprises a great portion of central QLD down to the southwestern portion of NSW, as well as the area along the northern portion of Alice Springs, NT and the northern tip of VIC. There are also several savannahs in WA specifically in the northern portion below the Kimberley region, the western coast along Pilbarra, and the area between Perth and the great deserts. There is also a small portion of grassland in between NT and SA including SA's south-central parts.

The climate here is the same as in the tropics with an almost equal number of dry and wet months. The main difference is that the tropics often consist of dense jungles while grass is the only plant that grows in the savannahs.

5. Temperate zone (Moderate climate) – the southern tip of SA belongs to the temperate zone. This mostly consists of the coastal areas along Streaky Bay, as well as the areas in and around Adelaide. Southern VIC, the southeastern coast of NSW including the entire Australian Capital Territory (ACT), a tiny portion of southern QLD, and Tasmania (TAS) also belong to this zone. These areas do not experience the extreme weather conditions that characterize the other zones.

Australia also goes through the four seasons. However, the pattern for these seasons is completely opposite that of the US and other countries in the northern hemisphere. The seasons fall under the following months:
- June to August – Winter
- September to November – Spring
- December to February – Summer
- March to May – Autumn/Fall

The winters are often cooler in the areas that fall under the temperate zone due to its relative proximity to the polar region.

Chapter 3: Sydney

Sydney is the capital of the state of New South Wales. It is the most densely populated city in Australia with a population count of 4.6 million people. This is the city where the first British settlers landed and subsequently founded the penal colony. It is also the same area where most of the Aborigines lived. Most of the colonial history discussed in Chapter 1 involves Sydney and the state of New South Wales.

While Sydney is a capital city with all the usual features – massive shopping centers, business districts, and sprawling residential areas – it is also surrounded by national parks, which then flow straight into the heart of the city. Head down to the harbor area and you will see bush still fringing it, as well as smaller parks scattered through the imposing buildings and into the suburbs. As a result, don't be surprised to see wild animals scampering throughout these areas, searching for fruits and other foods. You may even see an over-sized spider or two lurking in the corner of the houses, possums running over the roofs of houses and birds screeching from balconies. Indeed, Sydney may be an urban jungle but the native wildlife makes it just as wonderful as the natural one.

Sydney's harbor area gives the city its charm, defining the city itself. Exploring the city from the water is an experience all by itself. All you have to do is jump on a boat and you will discover there's so much more to the capital than what any travel guide can tell you. On either side of the river lies various attractions to experience, including a range of beaches where visitors can lie back, soak up the sun and socialize with others.

If you compare Sydney with other Australian cities, then you will discover it's completely different! Sydney is loud, energetic and busy. There are always firework displays held throughout the city all through the year, with vibrant nightclubs, cocktail bars and restaurants catering to all cuisines here. Add into the mix a great arts and cultural scene, and Sydney is certainly one of those destinations where you will find anything and everything you want!

3.1 Where to Go – Best Places for Sightseeing and Adventure

Sydney has a lot of tourist spots. Some of these spots date back to colonial times, while others are more recent. The must-see places include:

The Sydney Opera House – this is the most popular and the most recognizable Australian landmark. The location in itself is significant because of its role in the history of Sydney. Bennelong Point used to be the site of Fort Macquarie Tram Depot from 1902 until its demolition in 1958. Bennelong Point lies along the southern portion of Sydney Harbour. Its location ensures that the Opera House would be visible from all angles.

Tourists can sign up for guided tours that start at 9am and last until 5pm. The tours may entail certain fees depending on the event that may be included on it. The Sydney Opera House also has several theatres that play up to 40 shows per day. Getting a list of the shows is easy. All you need to do is visit the official website at www.sydneyoperahouse.com .

How to get there:
- Take any of the following buses: 333, 380, 392, 394, 396, and 399. Pick up point is at Martin Place Station on Stand C along Elizabeth Street. Landing point is at Circular Quay on Stand D along Young Street. From there, walk north and make a slight left turn on Alfred Street. Turn right onto Circular Quay E and walk straight until you reach the Opera Bar. The Opera House should already be visible from there.

The Rocks – history buffs are definitely going to have a feast at The Rocks. This is where the British first set foot in 1788 to establish the penal colony. The site is also rich in Aboriginal history since it was also one of the Gadigal's favorite hunting grounds. Unfortunately, the discovery of a campfire that is believed to have been built during the 1400s is probably the only trace left of Aboriginal presence on The Rocks.

Unlike the aboriginal history of the place, a number of British colonial structures are still in evidence on The Rocks. Most of the structures that date back to the early years were built through convict labor. Most of the buildings have been converted from their original purpose into restaurants, hotels, and other establishments. They are now also equipped with modern fixtures such as electricity and plumbing. However, the old-world charm of the buildings is still intact since these are protected under the Sydney heritage list.

How to get there:
- The best way to go is to walk from the CBD since it is a mere 900 meters away.

Bondi Beach – this is another one of Sydney's most popular attractions. Aside from swimming and taking colorful snapshots, avid surfers can enjoy some great surfing time at Bondi beach. Those who are new to the craft can sign up for lessons at some of the surfing schools in the area. While those who are not so interested in surfing can simply just lay back on the glistening white sand.

Who knows, you might even be lucky enough to catch a sight of amazing shelf clouds rolling into the city from the ocean just like the clouds that rolled in back in November of 2015.

Just a bit of trivia: Bondi is an aboriginal word. It roughly means the sound of the seawater breaking over the rocky promontories on one end of the beach.

How to get there:

- Take Bus 380 at Stand F on Martin Place Station along Elizabeth Street. The bus usually drops passengers off at a point on Campbell Parade that's adjacent to Hall Street. Bondi beach should be right across the street from the drop-off. Bus 380 leaves Martin Place on 30-minute intervals.

Sydney Olympic Park – the park is located at the western end of the city. It is often used as a venue for major sporting events, art exhibitions, trainings and workshops, and so much more. It was also the location of the 2000 Olympic Games, which is where the park got its name. Adults are not the only ones who can take advantage of the Park's offerings for further learning enhancement.

There is also a host of activities that kids can sign up for such as workshops on digital filmmaking or creative writing, sports training programs, and even pizza and/or pasta cooking sessions.

How to get there:

- Take the T1 tram at Wynyard Station and disembark at the T2 station in Strathfield. Walk a few meters to the Strathfield Bus Station in Everton Road and take bus number 525. Disembark at Dawn Fraser Avenue, which is about a 3-minute walk from the Olympic Park.

Taronga Zoo – this one is located at Sydney's northern portion. You don't have to travel all the way to the outback just to catch a glimpse of Australia's famous wild animals. With a population of more than 4,000 animals, it goes without saying that Taronga Zoo also holds some of the rarest animals in the country. These include the Goodfellow Tree Kangaroo, Tasmanian Devil, Australian Sea Lion, Southern Hairy-nosed Wombat and so much more.

The Zoo does not only serve as a holding place for these animals. It also conducts a host of programs that are designed to ensure that these species last for generations. There are breeding, conservation, and rehabilitation programs especially for the animals whose numbers are fast approaching extinction.

How to get there:
- Take the B247 bus as Wynyard Station and disembark at Bradleys Head Road. The zoo should be about 180 meters from the bus stop.

Sydney Olympic Park - located in the west of the city, Sydney Olympic Park is the city's key sporting and entertainment venue. Easily reached by train or ferry, it was renovated for the 2000 Olympic Games, which was held in Sydney, and as a result, the park has become recognizable for sporting and major events. However, it is also home to a variety of activities for all the family, stunning parks and a variety of different foods to sample.

Sydney Olympic Park features a range of venues, including the ANZ Stadium and the Sydney Showground, as well as venues designed for tennis, rugby, soccer and other sports. Throughout the year, various sporting competitions are hosted here. But don't think that only sports are performed here – Sydney Olympic Park puts on various musical concerts throughout the year, so whenever you come here, there's always something to see.

The Sydney Royal Easter Show is performed here. It began in 1998 and has been held here ever since. When it's on, the Sydney Royal Easter Show hosts a number of agricultural exhibitions and displays, fun rides for all the family and a number of other activities to enjoy.

The Sydney Olympic Park also gives visitors the chance to explore the fantastic Bicentennial Park, 40 hectares of sprawling wetlands, hills and stunning natural beauty. Popular with visitors and locals alike, there are several cycling and footpaths that take you throughout the park. Grab your blanket and picnic basket and enjoy watching the kids run around the adventure playground or just socialize with friends.

If you get hungry, there is an abundance of restaurants and cafes situated around the venue. Whether you want something quick and simple, or something a little more gourmet, there's something to suit all palates and budgets.

The Birds Australia Discover Centre -.is situated close to the Sydney Olympic Park, adjacent to the Newington Nature Reserve. Visitors can come here to learn more about the country's native birdlife, and features an impressive library and educational facilities. The center also provides highly engaging tours before heading next door to the nature reserve where you can see the creatures in their habitats.

There are two choices for the best times to visit Sydney. First is from the end of September up until the beginning of December and second is from the end of February to the beginning of

April. These are the months when the sun's heat isn't too unbearable.

3.2 Sydney: Where to Eat

Of course, a tour of the Sydney wouldn't be complete without sampling some of its rare and most popular dishes. For a worthwhile gastronomic experience, check out the establishments in the following locations:

Gardener's Lodge Café – this is the best place to enjoy some aboriginal cuisine along with a small dose of local history. It is located at Victoria Park, which is just 4-5 kilometers away from the Opera House and The Rocks. Eating and enjoying some great coffee is not the only reason why you have to visit the place. The restaurant is also one of Sydney's historical landmarks. The building is made of sandstone and has been standing since it was built by James Barnet in 1888.

Quay Restaurant – this restaurant is famous not only for its food but also for the spectacular views. Two of Sydney's famous landmarks can be seen from the restaurant: the Sydney Harbour Bridge and the Sydney Opera House. To learn more about their menu, as well as to book a reservation, go to http://www.quay.com.au.

Bennelong – this café is located right at the heart of the Sydney Opera House. It has 4 different dining levels for guests to choose from. Each level is designed to provide diners with a unique dining experience. The main restaurant opens for lunch and dinner. Lunch starts at 12 noon to 2pm Fridays to Sundays only and dinner starts at 6:30pm to 10pm daily. A 2-course lunch menu would normally cost around AUD$100, while a 3-course menu is around AUD$130. Dinner only serves 3-course menus that are worth around AUD$130.

For more information, check out their website at
http://www.bennelong.com.au.

Oscillate Wildly – don't be fooled by this restaurant's wild
name. It is actually one of the most romantic eating spots in
Sydney. It is the best choice for couples who want to enjoy an
intimate dinner in a quiet neighborhood after a long day of
adventures. Reservations can be made through their website at
http://www.oscillatewildly.com.au.

The View café – this is conveniently located inside the
Taronga Zoo. It offers a la carte dining and a great view of the
Sydney skyline, including an amazing view of the Sydney
Opera House. It has an extensive seafood menu, though there
are some non-seafood products as well. The View opens at
10am and closes at 4pm, with lunch served starting at
11:30am.

1802 Oyster Bar and Bistro - Coffin Bay Oysters are
famous to Sydney and there's no better place to sample them
that at the 1802 Oyster Bar and Bistro. If you're not a fan of
the delectable oysters, then you can feast on a wide variety of
other seafoods, all freshly caught from the coastline of the
Eyre Peninsular, renowned for its seafood. It is from here,
around the town of Coffin Bay, that the oysters are sourced
from, and are shipped to master chefs from all around the
world. Sit back, enjoy beautiful food with great service at the
1802 Oyster Bar and Bistro. **Address**: 61 Esplanade, Coffin
Bay, South Australia 5607

3.3 Where to Stay

There are many options for tourist accommodation in and around Sydney. Prices vary depending on the level of luxury and comfort provided by the establishment. Check out the following accommodation types in Sydney for your reference:

Four Seasons Hotel Sydney – this hotel offers great views of Sydney harbor, specifically the Sydney Opera House and Sydney Harbour Bridge. They offer several rate packages such as the Romance Package, Bed and Breakfast package, and so on. Expect to pay no less than AUD$290+ per night for a room at this hotel. For more information, check out their website at http://www.fourseasons.com/sydney or call +61 (2) 9250-3100.

Intercontinental Sydney – this has been serving Sydney's upper crust for more than three decades now. Its best feature is the wrap around terrace that offers guests an untarnished view of the harbor and everything that's in it. Expect to pay at least AUD$280+ per night. For more information check out http://www.icsydney.com.au or call +61 (2) 9253-9000. You can also send an email to sydney@interconsydney.com.

Best Western –Phillip Lodge Motel – this is often rated as a 3-star hotel in various reviews. It is located in the Ashfield suburb and is just a few kilometers away from the Sydney Olympic Park, as well as the Sydney Showgrounds. Some of its amenities include free parking and an outdoor swimming pool. Room rates are around AUD$93 to AUD$121 for standard rooms. For booking and reservations, check out https://www.bestwestern.com.au/sydney/hotels/bestwestern-ashfields-philip-lodge-motel/ or call +61 (2) 9797 9411.

Novotel Sydney Darling Harbour - Ideally located in Sydney's Central Business District, the Novotel Sydney Darling Harbour is a beautiful four star hotel offering great value for money and impressive facilities. Rooms are spacious and light, many of which feature outstanding views over the city. Rooms come with flat screen televisions with cable and in-house movies, and a well-equipped bathroom.

Guests can keep in shape at the hotel's fitness center, the outdoor tennis courts or swim off the pounds at the outdoor swimming pool. The hotel also boasts a fantastic selection of restaurants to enjoy. The Ternary Restaurant is a highly sophisticated setting in which guests can dine on beautifully prepared dishes. The Grill Kitchen and the Asian Kitchen offer great food and equally great atmospheres. For those who wish to socialize, the Wine War offers a good drinks menu featuring world-class wines, spirits and beers.

is ideally situated for those staying on business or leisure. The Harbourside Shopping Centre is a short three minute walk away, as well as the Wildlife Sydney Zoo, the National Maritime Museum and Sea Life Sydney Aquarium. There are good transport links into the heart of the city, or if you fancy the walk, it's only 15 minutes away on foot. **Address**: 100 Murray Street, Sydney CBD, 2009 Sydney.

There are also several campsites around Sydney for those who love the outdoors. Do note that the best campsites are often located a few miles outside of the Sydney CBD. Those who want to stay close to Bondi beach can also choose to stay in an affordable backpacking lodge.

Bondi Backpackers is considered to be the best campsite for tourists. It is located at the heart of the Bondi beach area, which means that guests can just walk to and from anywhere. A single room costs around AUD$60-120. The rates go up according to the size of the room. If you're interested in booking a reservation, just go to http://www.bondibackpackers.com.au or call +61 (0)2 9130 4660.

3.4 Sydney Nightlife

Sydney's nightlife is as vibrant as its daytime scene. This vibrancy is due to the fact that there are a number of nightclubs that cater to almost every type of partygoer. These include jazz bars, music clubs, comedy bars, bars that are exclusive for the LGBT community, and so on. These places are also scattered throughout the city, which means that there would always be a place for bored tourists to go regardless of where they're staying.

Some of the best spots include:

Civic Underground – this club is located at the underground level of the Civic Hotel along Pitt Street. It is about 10 to 15 minutes away from the CBD and buses ply the route every 10 minutes or so. Civic Underground is not just a mere nightclub. Tourists can go there to party, listen to some of the city's most popular DJs, or to enjoy some late night a la carte dining.

Marquee – in the world of nightclubs, Marquee belongs to the big leagues. It is often compared to the party venues in Las Vegas, complete with DJs, Gogo dancers and the works. If you want to get a glimpse of Sydney's showbiz personalities, Marquee is the best place to go to.

Goros - Japanese karaoke meet Sydney. Sydney, meet Japanese karaoke. Visitors, welcome to Goros! Goros is a fantastic Japanese-style karaoke full of drinks and an equally amazing atmosphere. Located in Central, the karaoke joint is housed in a former tailor's and has undergone several renovations. The first renovation got the job done but it still lacked the right feel. Just recently, it has undergone a second makeover which has resulted in the right atmosphere and character. Nowadays, it's swapped the dark feel to a low-lit, a spray of multi-colored neon lights, oriental lanterns and iconic bamboo touches, all around three outstanding karaoke booths. Get those vocal chords relaxed by sipping on a drink – or several if the idea of singing in public scares you – before belting out a Whitney Houston classic or Psy's Gangnam Style. You can even enjoy a few brands of Japanese drinks, such as Kirin, Sapporo or Asahi, to get you really in the mood. The bar even serves a variety of sakes for those really prepared for the whole Japanese karaoke shebang. For those who like their cocktails, Goros will not disappoint. The cocktail list features a fantastic range of cocktails – sour, sweet, ultra-sweet – to help you work up the courage to sing. Beers and ales are aplenty and there's a variety of snack plates to nibble on all through the night and into the small hours.

Address: 84 - 86 Mary Street, Surry Hills, Sydney, New South Wales 2010. **Telephone**: +61 2 9212 0214

If you're staying anywhere near Bondi Beach, then there shouldn't be any reason not to go out at night. The area's nightlife is also just as colorful as Sydney's. What's more interesting is that the nightclubs in Bondi are not as restricted by the late-night liquor ban in the CBD. This means that you can go hopping from The Anchor, to the Beach Road Hotel, to the White Revolver without having to worry about lock outs.

Chapter 4: Melbourne

Brief History of Melbourne

Melbourne is the second most populous city in Australia with a total population of 4.2 million as of 2015. It is the capital city of the state of Victoria and was founded in August of 1835. Just like Sydney, Melbourne has retained the name that the first British settlers gave it. However, unlike Sydney, Melbourne never served as penal colony. It was founded by free settlers who came from another established colony in Australia: Van Diemen's Land, now known as Tasmania.

But before these first British settlers set foot on Melbourne, the location where the city was built already played a significant role. It was an important place for gatherings of the different tribes of the Kalin nation. This is a fact that the City of Melbourne recognizes to this day. Several holidays and festivals are celebrated as a way of making amends for the injustice suffered by the Aborigines and Torres Strait Islanders at the coming of the European settlers.

Some of the well-known holidays include:
- National Sorry Day
- National Aboriginal and Islander Children's Day
- Mabo Day
- National Reconciliation Week

To this day, many Aboriginal clans and Torres Strait Islander people still converge in Melbourne for meetings and events. As a matter of fact, an organization was created by several members of the indigenous community that would facilitate the events in one gathering place. This organization is known as the Mullum Mullum Indigenous Gathering Place or MMIGP.

But the indigenous people are not the only ones who gather in Melbourne for sporting events and other festivals. Each year, loads of tourists converge in the city to experience its wonders.

4.1 Where to Go – Best Places for Sightseeing and Adventure

In order to say that you have truly experienced life in Melbourne, it is imperative that you go see the following sights:

The Queen Victoria Market – the market stands over 17 acres of land, which makes it the largest of its kind on this side of the equator. The market's history is as colorful as the produce that's displayed daily on many of its stalls. It was conceptualized in 1878. At one point, it served as a cemetery before being reverted back to its original purpose. Today, it is the busiest open market in Australia. Tourists who want to sample a taste of the freshest seafood, poultry, and meat products won't be disappointed by the Queen Vic's offerings.

How to get there:
- Take the train from any station in Melbourne. There are two points where you can disembark: either Melbourne Central Station on Elizabeth Street or Flagstaff Station on William Street. Then walk the rest of the way to Queen Vic's, which should take approximately 7 minutes.
- Take any tram that goes to Elizabeth Street or Williams Street. These are mostly the tams numbered 19, 55, 57, and 59. They can alight either at Stop 7 or Stop 9 and then walk due north to the market.
- Take the Visitor Shuttle and disembark at stop number 8.

National Gallery of Victoria – also referred to as the NGV, is the leading museum in Australia, both in age and eminence.

The NGV has been around since 1861. It houses an extensive collection of ancient and modern art from all around the world. It also holds an extensive collection of Aboriginal art such as paintings that date back to the 1800s.

The gallery's collection is so extensive that the items have been distributed to two separate locations: the Ian Potter Centre: NGV Australia and NGV International. Both sites open at 10am daily from Sundays to Saturdays and close at 5pm. They are also closed on Christmas Day, as well as on Good Friday.

How to get there:
- NGV International is situated along St Kilda Road. This means that visitors can take any of the trams that ply the St Kilda Road route. They can disembark at the Arts Precinct. The same tram numbers can also be taken to get to the Ian Potter Centre.
- Gallery can also take the train to NGV International. However, since they would be alighting at the station on Flinders Street, they might as well check out The Ian Potter Centre first. They can then cross the bridge over to NGV International.
- Visitors who are unsure of the tram depots or train stations can also opt for a taxi.

Port Campbell National Park – this is one of the best places to go to for some sightseeing. The first thing you should check out is a series of rock formations known as The Twelve Apostles. The rocks have been standing for millions of years, originally starting out as part of the mainland. Erosion caused them to be separated until they now stand like watchful sentinels on the beach. Tourists can get close to the rocks to appreciate their magnificent beauty or go high up on the cliffs.

They should be able to enjoy the entire panorama from the top of the cliffs, as well as get some amazing souvenir shots.

The Park also has many other spots that would make it worth any tourist's time. There's The Grotto, Gibson's Steps, the Loch Ard Gorge, and London Arch. Visitors can also enjoy a wide variety of outdoor activities in various areas scattered around the 4,300-acre park. You can take the kids camping, fishing, horseback riding, and so much more.

How to get there:
- Take the train the Southern Cross station. Disembark at Camperdown and then hop onto a bus that's headed towards the Timboon-Curdievale Road. From there, hop onto a taxi and have it drop you off at the Park entrance. Travel time would take about 4-5 hours so be prepared to leave Melbourne early

Melbourne's Beaches – Melbourne sits right at the center of Port Phillip, which means that it has a lengthy coastline. This also means that there is a long list of beaches for tourists to choose from. The most famous among these beaches is St Kilda Beach, which is located just a few miles to the west of St Kilda Road. It offers a wide variety of activities including swimming, of course. The site also has a pier where visitors can take romantic walks while basking under the warm Melbourne sun.

All the other beaches in Melbourne have its own distinct charm. Tourists can also engage in various water activities in any of these beaches such as boating and sailing. Non water-related activities that can be enjoyed at some of these beaches include rollerblading, biking, jogging, and so on.
How to get there:

- Take the line 96 tram at Stop 125 and then disembark at Canterbury Road Stop 133. Head left towards The Esplanade and get into St Kilda Beach from any direction. The other beaches can be reached either by tram, train, or car.

Yarra Valley – most tour agencies often incorporate the Dandenong Ranges on a tour of the Yarra Valley due to its proximity. The name of the valley is believed to have come from the other name by which the Wurundjeri tribe was referred to: the Yarra Yarra. This tribe is the traditional watchmen of the Yarra valley. Visitors have the option of immersing in Aboriginal culture once they visit the Valley.

The Yarra Valley is also quite well-known for its wine. There are vineyards as far as the eye can see, most of which have been around since the early 1800's. These vineyards serve as great venues for various events, especially weddings and romantic getaways.

Tip: the Yarra Valley is so huge that it encompasses at least 4 major towns. Each of these towns has its own unique offerings for tourists. It's best to plan a trip that would allow you to stay for at least 2 to 3 days. Accommodations can be booked at any of the vineyards. This should also give you enough time to explore the nearby Dandenong range.

How to get there:
- By car. This is the most recommended mode of transport to the Yarra Valley from Melbourne CBD and vice versa. This is also the best way to get around the Yarra Valley if you haven't booked a travel agency's services.

Travelling to the Yarra Valley takes approximately an hour either from Melbourne City Centre or from the Melbourne Airport. If you have booked accommodations with any of the local hotels, then it might be possible to request for a pick up from the airport or at any point in Melbourne. It is best to verify this with the establishment first.

Abbotsford Convent - When in Melbourne, it would be a sacrilege if you don't pay a visit to Abbotsford Convent. Located on the edge of the inner city, it is a great place to soak up Melbourne's artistic scene. Visitors can view and participate in a variety of different performances, workshops, events and classes, from writing to painting to illustration. The gardens are a masterpiece of art by themselves, the perfect place for relaxation and inspiration, as are the well laid-out art galleries where visitors can explore. Don't forget lunch – you can sample delectable Japanese cuisine, a vegetarian curry or café delights.

How To Get There
- **Address**: 1 St Heliers Street, Melbourne, Victoria, 3600

Australian Tapestry Workshop - Adelaide is renowned for her arts and cultural scene and no better can this be experienced than at the Australian Tapestry Workshop. Also known as the ATW, it boasts a reputation for being one of the global leaders in modern tapestries.

The ATW opened its doors to the public in 1976 and is the only one of its kind in the entire country. There are only a few around the world that produce handmade tapestries. The workshop is housed within a beautiful building dating back to the latter part of the 19th century, a prime example of Gothic-free Victorian buildings.

Since its founding, the ATW has produced over 500 tapestries of all sizes, ranging from the palm of your hand to those built on a gigantic scale, using the best Australian wool. The wool is dyed in the workshop, a stunning range of 370 colors. The weavers come, not just only from Australia, but from all over the world, famous for their exceptional skills, to create masterpieces which captivate the senses and the imagination.

Throughout the decades, there have been a number of artists from all over the world who have worked with the ATW. These include Arthur Boyd, Jorn Utzon, Sally Smart and Brook Andrew.

The tapestries created at the ATW have been proudly displayed at various exhibitions and displays across Australia and the rest of the world, as well as within private collections. You can see some hanging at the Great Hall of Parliament House in Canberra. The Sydney Opera House, the National Gallery of Victoria, and the Melbourne Recital Centre. There are also some displayed within nine Australian embassies around the world. For those interested in the history of tapestries, the ATW hosts exhibitions, workshops, tours, classes and talks. Visitors can even book a weaving class and there are classes for children as well.

How To Get There
- 262- 266 Park Street, South Melbourne, Victoria, 3205

The best time to go on a tour of Melbourne is during the temperate months of March to May and September to

November. Not only is the climate favorable during these months, there also tends to be less tourists around.

March to May is autumn in Melbourne, which means that the city would be alight with the vibrant colors of the season. There are also several festivals held during this time, including the Future Music Festival, Melbourne Food and Wine Festival, and Australia's Formula One Grand Prix.

September to November is springtime, which means that the city's natural colors are just starting to come out. Timing a visit in September means that you can still catch the final moments of the Winter Festival and the Writers' Festival, which both start in August and end in September.

4.2 Where to Eat

Melbourne has a lot of restaurants that not only offer great food to its diners, but also the most scenic views. Some of the options include:

Anchorage Restaurant – diners eat with the relaxing view of Hobsons Bay in the background. It is also one of the more interesting establishments in the city as it is located in a refurbished boat shed. The exterior and interior designs of the place are carefully designed to maintain its rustic boat shed ambience. Diners can go to http://www.anchorage.com.au to reserve the best seats with a view or call +61 (03) 9397 7799.

Zonzo – this is the place to go if you want rows upon rows of vineyards as the backdrop to your dining experience while simultaneously feasting on authentic Italian cuisine. It is located within the Yarra Valley and is a popular site among the locals for weddings and special events. Zonzo has also won numerous awards throughout the years. Check out their website at http://www.zonzo.com.au or call +61 (03) 9730 2500.

Pure South Dining – this restaurant is located along the southern banks of the Yarra River. It offers a taste of modern Australian cuisine with ingredients that are 100% fresh from the paddocks. Diners also get a great view of the surrounding metropolitan area, with Melbourne's tallest skyscrapers serving as the backdrop for their photos. Reservations can be made at http://www.puresouth.com.au or call +61 3 9699 4600.

Sky High Mount Dandenong – this is the place to be if you want to take some really amazing photos of the sunset. The varying shades of red, pink, and orange are offset by the blinking lights of the city at twilight. A lot of Melbournians actually go to Sky High just for the view. But those who go there to dine won't be disappointed since the food is also excellent. Check out http://www.skyhighmtdandenong.com.au or call +61 (03) 9751 0443 for reservations.

Eleonore's Restaurant – the restaurant is located within the confines of the historic Chateau Yering, which dates back to the early years of the Yarra Valley wine industry. This history can be felt from the restaurant's interior design, as well as from the country vibe that the surrounding lands provide. The Chateau also has a hotel so tourists can book a room there if they're planning to explore Yarra Valley for a couple of days.

Reservations can be made at http://www.chateauyering.com.au. You can also call +61 3 9237 3333 or the toll free number 1800 237 333.

Il Pom Italian - If you fancy a taste of Italy within Melbourne, there's no better place to go than Il Pom Italian. Whether its lunch or dinner, the food here is absolutely delicious, especially when dining al fresco underneath the red umbrellas. **Address**: 2 Swanston Street, Melbourne, Victoria 3000

4.3 Where to Stay

There are hundreds of hotels, motels, and whatnot scattered around Melbourne for every type of tourist to stay in. The following are just some of the options that you can choose from depending on the allotted budget for accommodation:

Park Hyatt Hotel – this 5-star hotel is located right at the heart of the CBD, which is always a good starting point for touring the city and its surrounds. It has everything that you can expect from a 5-star hotel, including the option to personalize the amenities in their rooms. Check out http://melbourne.park.hyatt.com for room availability or call their toll free number at 1-800-633-7313. Rates vary according to room/suite type.

Habitat HQ – this hostel is located along St. Kilda Road so it would be a good place to stay for tourists who are planning to spend a lot of time at the beach. It has a communal space and a beer garden and guests are entitled to free breakfast. Most of the rooms also have unique wallpapers hanging on its walls. You can view photos of the rooms and book a reservation at http://www.habitathq.com.au or call 1800 202 500.

Southern Ocean Villas – this is a great option for tourists who wish to enjoy the sights at the Port Campbell National Park for more than just a few hours. Even guests who don't plan to stay overnight can book a room at the Villa. It could serve as their base for leaving their extra baggage and for freshening up before heading back to the city. Rates vary depending on the size of the Villa that you rent. For more information, go to http://www.southernoceanvillas.com or call +61 (03) 5598 4200.

The Hotel Windsor - The Hotel Windsor was established in 1883 and boasts a rich legacy as the city's grandest hotel. The hotel holds the most awards for its excellent facilities and amenities, as well as for its superb accommodation and attentive service. The accommodation is designed to be inviting and light, with all the latest amenities. Great views await those who stay here, with many overlooking the Parliament House and the Treasury Gardens. The Hotel Windsor is ideally situated, being close to several key attractions including the Melbourne Cricket Ground, with good transport links close by. **Address**: 111 Spring Street, Melbourne, Victoria 3000

4.4 Melbourne Nightlife

The vibrancy of Melbourne's nightlife is comparable to its festivals. Most of the bars and nightclubs also possess unique eye-catching names that make them hard for party-animals to resist. Some of the most popular spots include:

Naked for Satan – don't take this name literally. Nobody gets naked for anybody inside the premises of this club. To understand where the name came from, check out http://www.nakedforsatan.com.au. It's located along Brunswick Street in Fitzroy. Bookings can only be made by cal+61 (03) 9416 2238 or sending an email to naked@nakedforsatan.com.au

Therapy Nightclub – the only therapy you'd get from this place is the kind provided by drunken revelry. This nightclub is located at the Crown Entertainment Complex in Southbank. It's a favorite hangout for celebrities and other famous personalities. For bookings call 1300 723 391 or check out http://www.level3atcrown.com.au for more information.

M.O.O – this is perfect for men who are curious about what happens inside a gentleman's club. M.O.O. is short for Money Order Office, which is the original name of the place where the nightclub now stands. This faux gentleman's club is equipped with all the necessities, including high-backed leather chairs and a dimly-lit but opulent ambience. Reservations can be made by calling +61 (03) 9639-3020.

Yah Yah's -Yah Yah's is one of Melbourne's funkiest underground nightclubs that is often overlooked by the glitzy lights of surrounding clubs. However, don't let these lights outshine Yah Yah's own glittering success. Located in Fitzroy, visitors head into the club via a dark street entrance. Welcoming a variety of different characters, this is quite a quirky place to hang out. It's much quieter as well, but this makes it great as you don't have to weave in and out for ages just trying to get somewhere that would normally take you a minute to do so. As soon as you enter, you'll be greeted by a warm and friendly atmosphere, as though it's full of friends.

Don't be quick to the judge the place when you hear the music, it's full of stuff that you might not be familiar with, which only gives it charm. It's a little bit quirky, a little bit strange, and completely fun. Think of it as commercial pop with a twist of indie fun. When it comes to drinks, the main flavor seems to be beer. Don't expect fancy cocktails or wine. There's a seating section to one side of the bar, perfect for those who want to socialize and engage in conversation. The bathrooms are located at the back of the bar, close to the courtyard where smoking is permitted. The dance floor isn't massive, but it's perfect for those who want to get their groove on.

Address: 99 Smith Street. Fitzroy, Melbourne.

Chapter 5: Brisbane

Brief History of Brisbane

Brisbane is Australia's third largest city with a population count of 2.3 million people as of 2015. It is also the capital city of the state of Queensland. Just like many other cities in the country, Brisbane used to be inhabited by Aboriginal tribes for thousands of years before they were displaced by the Europeans. Specifically, two clans called the river its home: the Jagera and the Turrbal people. Unfortunately, their numbers were severely decimated not just by disease, but also by the alcoholic drinks that the white men provided in abundance.

Just like Sydney, Brisbane was also settled as a penal colony in 1825. However, unlike Sydney, the convicts that were settled in Brisbane were not fresh off the boat from England. Instead, these were convicts who had to be removed from the Sydney penal colony for secondary offenses. The city is located along the banks of the Brisbane River.

5.1 Where to Go – Best Places for Sightseeing and Adventure

The Lone Pine Koala Sanctuary – the sanctuary stands on 44 acres of land and is home not only to Koalas but also to several other native Australian wildlife. There are Tasmanian devils, wombats, kangaroos, one lone platypus, echidnas, and many other species at the zoo. Visitors to the sanctuary not only get to take a close look at the Koalas, they also get the chance to hold these cute furry animals for a few photo ops.

How to get there:
- Take bus number 430 from the station along Queen Street. This journey should take approximately 45 minutes and could cost around AUD$7.20.

Take the Mirimar Cruise ship at South Bank. The ship usually leaves the pontoon at the Cultural Centre at around 10am. It gets back from the Koala Sanctuary at 1:45pm. Don't forget to enjoy the view of the metropolitan Brisbane area from the river while you're at it

Coochiemudlo Island – this tiny island offers a chance for families to stay on the beach for as long as they like. They can check in at any of the island's guest cottages for however long they might wish to stay. The island's main attraction is the red rock that protrudes along its southwest shore, whence the name of the island came from.

Aside from a small patch of mangroves on one side, the entire island is covered with pristine white sand.

How to get there:

- Take the national bus from Brisbane and alight at the jetty along Victoria point.
- If traveling by car, drive to Cleveland Road. Turn left at Benfer Road then drive straight through to the jetty at Victoria Point. Take the ferry from there. The first ferry leaves at 5am and subsequent trips are scheduled in 30-minute intervals. The last ferry trip is at 11pm.
- Take the barge. This one might not be too reliable since there is no fixed schedule. However, if you do catch a barge before the next ferry comes in, then best to take that trip to have more time exploring the island.

Botanic Gardens at Mount Coot-tha – this is the most extensive botanic garden in Brisbane. It contains at least 10 thematic displays. These displays include the Japanese Garden, the Bonsai House, the Exotic Rainforest display, and a lot more. Aside from these garden displays, visitors can also enjoy a number of relaxing activities such as twilight yoga classes and story-time for kids.

The Sir Thomas Brisbane (from whom the city's name was taken) Planetarium is right across the street from the garden. Be sure to check it out before you leave the area. There are also several interesting locations in the vicinity, such as a walking track along the JC Slaughter Falls and an Aboriginal Art Trail that span at least 1.5 kilometers.

How to get there:

- Take bus number 471, which usually picks passengers up at Adelaide Street in the CBD. It usually drops passengers off right at the entrance to the gardens.

- Drive a car along Milton Rd on State Route 32. The drive is usually pretty straightforward until you reach the foothills of Mount Coot-tha.

The Brisbane CBD – there's no need to get out of the CBD just to immerse in Brisbane's history and culture. That's because the CBD also has some of the oldest buildings not only in Queensland, but in the entire country as well. The best way to see all of CBD's top attractions is to go on foot. You'll surely find rare architectural treasures such as the Parliament House, the Museum of Brisbane located inside the Brisbane City Hall, and so much more. The sightseeing tour on foot should also take you to the City Botanic Gardens, The Queens Gardens, and the historic King George Square.

Take a few detours on some side streets to see a lot of other buildings that belong to the Queensland Heritage List. Some of these buildings are government-owned, while others are owned by private entities such as churches, schools, and hotels. Some of the more interesting side streets include Ann Street, Charlotte Street, and Margaret Street. In case you get hungry, then just slip into any of the restaurants that you'll definitely encounter along the way.

How to get there:
- No need to worry about transportation if you're staying at a hotel in the CBD. The only thing to think about is on how to read a map of the CBD and how to choose the best starting point.

Kangaroo Point Cliffs – this is the best way to enjoy the outdoors without straying far away from Brisbane's CBD. All you need to do is cross the Brisbane River. The cliffs are actually not natural structures since they were created after extensive mining work was done on the rocks for use in building. Once there, visitors get the chance to climb the historic Story Bridge right to the very top. There, they can take in the view of the city from a high vantage point.

The more adventurous tourist can also take advantage of the chance to scale the 18-meter-high Kangaroo Point Cliffs. Even inexperienced climbers can try it out since the cliffs fall under the recreational climbing category.

How to get there:
- Drive a car from George Street at the CBD straight through to the Pacific Motorway and onwards to Woollongabba. Continue on from State Route 15 toward Kangaroo Point.
- Take the ferry at North Quay 1 terminal.

March to May is also the best time to visit Brisbane since it would also be autumn there. But tourists may also be interested in booking trips that coincide with some of the city's festivals.

5.2 Where to Eat

Just like any other establishment in the major cities in Australia, Brisbane's dining facilities often mix history with pleasure. Some of the establishments you might want to try out include:

Lone Pine Riverside Cafe – this lies right across from the koala sanctuary. Visitors to the sanctuary don't have to worry about freshening up for a formal lunch since the café has an informal atmosphere. Guests just need to buy food from the kiosk and then bring it over to the communal eating area. The river, the trees, the blue sky and the mansions that gracefully adorn the other side of the riverbank all serve as the backdrop for a relaxing family outing.

The Wishing Well Café – located at Victoria Point, this quaint café dates back to WWI. The café's name is derived from the well, which originally served as a source of water for American soldiers. Aside from its history, the café is popular for its homely and affordable meals and its selection of teas. It is also a popular spot among dog owners.

Red Rooster Indooroopilly – the name of the place speaks for itself: it is a chicken place. Its primary menu item is roast chicken though there is also a vast selection of other menu items to choose from. The place is also a stone's throw away from Mount Coot-tha. Check out http://www.redrooster.com.au or call 07 3378 7810 for inquiries.

Customs House – located at the heart of the CBD along the Brisbane River, this establishment is one of Queensland's heritage buildings. Its name refers to the building's history as the place where customs duty used to be collected. It now houses the University of Queensland with the Customs House restaurant incorporated within. Diners can choose to eat inside the historic building or al fresco with a great view of the river at sunset. Reservations can be made at http://www.customshouse.com.au/restaurant or by calling +61 7 3365 8921.

Summer House – after sending a hectic day at Kangaroo Point Cliffs, tourists can proceed to the Summer House for a relaxed meal. The menu mostly consists of modern Australian cuisine with a few twists here and there. But the one thing that patrons love about the place is that it allows them to forget the fast flow of their lifestyles even for just a few hours. For more information, check out http://www.summerhousebrisbane.com.au or call +61 (07) 3891 7005.

5.3 Where to Stay

Your budget should be able to cover any of the following accommodations:

Stamford Plaza Brisbane – this 5-star hotel is located on the southern portion of the Brisbane CBD. Its upscale facilities include a spa, an outdoor swimming pool, and a barber/beauty shop. Guests are also treated to great views of the Brisbane skyline and the Brisbane River. Its proximity to many of Brisbane's popular tourist spots means that you wouldn't have to travel far just to see the sights. For reservations and booking information, check out http://www.stamford.com.au/spb or call +61-7 3221 1999.

Kookaburra Inn – this is a great option for backpackers who don't want to spend their entire budget on a 5-star luxury. The inn is located in Spring Hill near the river and is within walking distance from the City Centre. Go to http://kookaburra-inn.com.au or call 617 3832 1303 for booking inquiries.

Regatta Hotel – this hotel has been standing proud for more than a century. It has retained its old-world splendor while simultaneously embracing the comforts of modernity. Checking into the Regatta Hotel is like travelling back in time and witnessing all the important historical events that the hotel has borne witness to. For reservations, go to http://www.regattahotel.com.au or call +61 (07) 3871 9595.

5.4 Brisbane Nightlife

Brisbane is home to Australia's first-ever entertainment precinct located in Fortitude Valley. It is popularly known among locals as simply 'the valley' and it contains everything that a tourist might want or need for nighttime entertainment. Aside from night spots, the valley also has a commercial area where some of the country's leading retailers showcase their products.

Despite its booming nightlife, or maybe because of it, the valley is one of three Drink Safe Precincts in Queensland. This means that there is increased police presence during the busiest drinking nights and there is increased cooperation between various emergency sectors.

Chapter 6: Perth

Brief History of Perth

Perth comes close to Brisbane in population count with at least 2.2 million people as of 2015. Perth is the third colony to be founded by the British in Australia. The first settlement was established in 1829 by Captain James Stirling as the center for administration of the so-called Swan River Colony. Perth sits on the southern tip of Western Australia in an area of land that is often referred to as the Swan Coastal Plain.

The fact that it lies so close to the water means that Perth was also inhabited by Aborigines whose primary staple was fish and seafood for most of the year. Perth's original inhabitants were the Bibbullmun, which consisted of at least 23 states. These people thrived in the Swan river area for thousands of years thanks to its abundant wildlife. Unlike the Aborigines of Sydney, Melbourne, and Brisbane, the Bibbullmun did not give up their rights to the Swan river area without a fight.

Hence, the war that became known as the Battle of Pinjarra was fought in 1834. Unfortunately, the Aborigines were no match for British firepower. What started out as a battle soon turned into a massacre. A monument has since been erected at McLarty Road to commemorate the unfortunate event.

6.1 Where to Go – Best Places for Sightseeing and Adventure

Perth is mostly sunny with a few rainy days now and then. This type of climate makes it an ideal city to go sightseeing at almost any time of the year. Listed below are just some of the places that tourists can go to all year round:

Adventure World – this amusement park is located just a few kilometers outside of Perth's CBD. It has been standing on the shores of Bibra Lake since November 1982. The park has undergone a lot of reconstruction ever since it opened and it now has some of the most thrilling rides in the country. After its final renovation in the early 2000's, Adventure World has consistently been receiving a lot of positive reviews both from Aussies and tourists alike.

The park is open on Thursdays through Mondays from 10am to 5pm and is closed on Tuesdays and Wednesdays.

How to get there:
- Take the train at the Perth Underground Station on Platform 2 and alight at Cockburn Station Platform 2. Then take the line 520 bus at Cockburn Station Stand 10 and alight at the junction of Progress drive and Gwilliam drive. Walk over from Progress Drive to Adventure World, which should take no more than 2 minutes max.
- Take a cab from Perth to Adventure World. This is a more expensive option but it is better for groups travelling together and could split the fare.
- Drive a car. This option may be preferable for families who are travelling with small children and a lot of

luggage in tow. Parking space at the park is totally free. Families can also hire gazebos for the day so that they'd have a place to leave their belongings at while they go out and have fun.

Swan River – the river was first discovered by Dutch explorers in 1697. They named it the Black Swan River after the flocks of black swans that used to abound in the area. However, much like the Dutch discovery of other Australian cities, they never stayed in Swan River for long. It wasn't until the arrival of the British that the first European colony was established along the shores of the Swan River.

Today, the river plays a big role in the lifestyle of Western Australians especially those who are living in Perth. People go there to swim, fish, and do all sorts of water sports. Unlike other rivers that are connected to major urban areas, the Swan River has managed to remain free of pollutants to this day.

How to get there:
- Walking is the best method for getting around this area.

Perth Zoo – the zoo stands on 41 acres of land and has been on operating since 1898. The zoo started out with a small collection of European animals. It has since grown and now holds 1100 animals from at least 190 species. Aside from keeping animals for display, the Perth Zoo is also active in animal conservation work. It has breeding programs in place for various native Australian species such as the numbat, Western Swamp Tortoise, several frog species, and a lot more.

The zoo opens daily from 9am to 5pm. It closes during 3 national holidays, which are Australia Day, Christmas Day, and Good Friday.

How to get there:

- Take bus number 30 or 31 at the bus station in Wellington Street and alight right in front of the zoo. Another option is to take bus number 34. Both of these buses are also accessible from the Esplanade Busport.
- Take the ferry at the Barrack Street jetty and alight at the Mends Street ferry located in the southern part of Perth. Walk a few kilometers from there to the zoo.
- Hail a cab from anywhere in Perth and alight right in front of the zoo entrance.
- Drive a car. Parking fees at the zoo normally depends on the length of your stay.

Perth's Beaches – Perth has a long line of beaches that stretch out from one end of its coastline to the other. The characteristics of each vary according to its location. There are beaches that are sheltered from waves and strong winds, which make it a good spot for families with small children to hang out in. These include Sandtrax beach and Port Beach.

How to get there:

- Depending on which beach you want to visit first, you can either walk from the CBD, take the tram, the bus, or the train.

Caversham Wildlife Park – this is a privately-owned park that holds a vast collection of animals, including a large number of native Australian animals. Visitors are given a chance to experience being up close with the animals. Those who are lucky enough may also get the chance to feed the animals and hold them for some photo ops. Some of the more exotic animals in the park include the Water Buffalo, Wedge Tailed Eagle, Rufus Bettong, and the Long-nosed Potoroo.

How to get there:

- The quickest way to get there is via train. Take the Midland Line at the Perth Station and disembark at Midland Station in Bassendean. From there, take bus number 955 and disembark at the junction of Lord Street and Youle-Dean Road. Walk from there towards the Park.

In general, Perth gets up to 300 days of sunny weather. This means that the best time to visit the city is anytime you're available. The Mediterranean climate of the city makes it easier for tourists to plan their itineraries according to the specific Perth festival they want to take part in.

6.2 Where to Eat

From fine dining to laid-back and informal, Perth has it all.

Incontro – this fine dining restaurant completes Perth's Mediterranean vibe. It also provides diners with a spectacular view of the city and the Swan River. Check out their menu at http://www.incontro.com.au or call (08) 9474 5566 to book a table.

Red Cabbage Food and Wine – this is another fine dining restaurant that also has a great view. It serves sophisticated modern Australian cuisine. To learn more about the menu, go to http://redcabbagefoodandwine.com.au or call (08) 9367 5744 for inquiries and reservations.

Kuditj Café – this is owned and managed by Aborigines and serves authentic bush tucker (Aboriginal) food. It is located in a building that has borne a lot of Perth's Aboriginal history. Despite its historic value, the café is nondescript and quite easy to miss unless you know that it stands exactly where it is. The staff consists entirely of Aboriginal students who are being trained so that they would qualify for jobs in the hospitality industry.

Gourmet Food Pass - The Gourmet Food Pass is the ideal place to visit if you are a traveler with a taste for fine dining. Here, diners can enjoy a fine whiskey or a delicious cocktail as you dine on a delectable dish. Popular with locals and visitors alike, the Gourmet Food Pass is one dining experience you don't want to miss out on. **Address**: Barrack Square Riverside Drive, Perth, Western Australia 6000

For more information on this highly interesting café, go to http://www.kuditj.com.au or call (08) 9228 0614 for inquiries.

6.3 Where to Stay

Just like any other developed city, Perth has a vast selection of accommodation types that tourists can choose from. Some of your options include:

The Vines Resort and Country Club – staying here is like vacation in itself where you don't have to do anything all day except play golf and go to the spa. It also has an outdoor pool, tennis courts, squash courts, a gym and dining facilities that are renowned for its sophistication. Guests can view photos of the resort at https://www.vines.com.au or call +61 (8) 9297 3000 for inquiries.

The Richardson Hotel and Spa – this is one of the most luxurious boutique hotels in Perth. It is also strategically placed in a location that is within walking distance of the CBD and a few other destinations around Perth. The hotel is also famous for its world-class Spa, which also includes a gym and a pool. Reservations and inquiries can be made at http://www.therichardson.com.au or by calling 61 (8) 9217 8888.

Hotel Northbridge – located at the suburb of Northbridge, this hotel is quite popular among backpackers. The rooms are clean and bottled water is provided for 2 guests per room free. The hotel also has a restaurant that serves some great food, as well as a bar that regularly hold groove karaoke every Friday. Check out their website at http://www.hotelnorthbridge.com.au or call 61 (08) 9328 5254 for inquiries.

The Terrace Hotel Perth - Located in the center of the West End district in Perth's CBD, the Terrace Hotel Perth is a fantastically stunning hotel situated in equally as impressive settings. This is the crème de la crème of Perth's accommodations, directed at the prestigious traveler who delights in high-class rooms, great entertainment, the full smorgasbord of facilities and amenities and a stay, which is tailored to the individual. Accommodation at the Terrace Hotel Perth is luxurious, spacious and designed with the comfort of the traveler in mind. Featuring all the latest gadgets and technology, the 15 suites are exquisitely decorated and furnished with Egyptian cotton sheets, televisions and iPads. En suite bathrooms are designed in gorgeous black marble with free-standing deep baths and showers. Location wise, the Terrace Hotel Perth is well suited for those who need to be in the heart of things. Centrally located, visitors only need to walk a short distance to be surrounded by a range of restaurants, bars, boutiques and transport links. The Terrace Hotel Perth offers a fine dining experience with restaurants, which offer a variety of delectable delights from all over the world. **Address**: 237 St George's Terrace, Perth, Western Australia 6000

Each of these accommodations has its pros and cons, including its proximity to certain areas. For instance, a backpackers' hotel in Northbridge is advantageous because it is within the same vicinity as Perth's Chinatown and some of the best exotic restaurants in the city. But then it is a few kilometers away from the CBD and the beach so you would have to take public transport to get there.

6.4 Perth Nightlife

Perth's colorful nightlife mostly revolves around three suburbs: Fremantle, Northbridge, and Subiaco. The close proximity of the clubs is one reason why a lot of tourists who have been to the city before often prefer to stay in any of Northbridge's backpacker hostels. Some of the more interesting establishments in Northbridge include:

The Bird – a favorite gathering place for artists and musicians. The place is also decorated with birds of all shapes and sizes and in a wide variety of poses and settings.

Mechanics Institute – rooftop bar whose patrons mostly consist of laid-back Aussies.

Sneaky Tony's – gives off a New York City vibe.

Ambar Nightclub - The sounds of the underground await you at the Ambar Nightclub, where reality seems surreal and the surreal seems crazily real. Relaxed and a little nutty, the Ambar Nightclub is a popular club for locals and those passing through who just want to kick back, enjoy a night out and go dancing. Opening late and closing even later, the Ambar Nightclub is located in the eastern part of Perth's Central Business District, but first you have to find it. It's actually situated in a little alley that screams unsavory, with only the door stating as to what lies within. Head inside and it almost reminds you of a cave, but with a seating area, snooker tables, a bar and dance area. The lighting and décor are somewhat strange, done in reds and yellows. Music wise, the club plays a range of genres but all within the techno, electro and house categories. For those that like soul, R&B and contemporary pop, this isn't really going to be the place for you. The music is exceptionally loud, the drinks flowing and the mood high. This is a popular place for those just come of drinking age so expect a few antics. Drinks are quite reasonable and there's a cover fee to get in, although this changes depending on the DJ is for that night. Once you're in, though, it's an energetic place where dancing is encouraged. **Address**: 104 Murray Street, Perth, WA

Fremantle's most popular nightclub is the Little Creatures, which was established on the same spot as the brewery that supplies it beer.

Chapter 7: Adelaide

Brief History of Adelaide

Adelaide has a population count of 1.30 million people as of 2015. This makes it the fifth most populous city in the country. The first British settlement in Adelaide was established in 1836 with the sole purpose of creating a colony of free settlers. Just like the other major cities, Adelaide was founded on the banks of a major source of water. In this case, the settlement was established on the River Torrens.

This means that Aboriginal communities had once again been extinguished to make way for the white man. The Kauran People were the original inhabitants of this part of the land.

If Sydney is big, loud and brash, then Adelaide is her sophisticated cousin who is always dressed to impressed. Adelaide retains a colonial feel, although one without the negative aspects which came from colonization. Along with this old world feel, the city also boasts a vibrant multi-cultural atmosphere, especially when it comes to the countless restaurants and eateries that are spread out. When it comes to nightlife, Adelaide's shy personality fades away with the setting sun and out comes a vibrant character. Numerous nightclubs, bars and other entertainment venues can be found throughout Adelaide, some hidden amongst the many church spires and down unsuspecting lanes and alleys.

7.1 Where to Go – Best Places for Sightseeing and Adventure

North Terrace Cultural Precinct – if your purpose in going to Adelaide is to immerse in a world of arts and culture, then the North Terrace Cultural Precinct is the right place to be at. The North Terrace is one long stretch of highway starting from the A21 in the west and ending along the junction of East Terrace and Botanic Road in the east. Along this stretch of highway are some of the country's most iconic cultural landmarks.

These landmarks include the Government House, the South Australian Institute Building, the State Library of South Australia, the Migration Museum, and the Art Gallery of South Australia. With the sole exception of the Migration Museum, all of these buildings date back to the mid- to late 1800's.

How to get there:
North Terrace is accessible from many points across the city. Also, most of the buildings are situated at a small distance from each other. This means that the mode of transportation that you choose depends on the building that you first want to explore. In most cases, a car or a taxi is often the best option.

- Take the connector bus with route numbers 98 and 99. These buses are free and they run on 30-minute intervals.
- Take the tram and alight at the tram stop on Bank Street. The Parliament building lies across the tram and the Government Building lies a few meters to the left and across the street from the Parliament building. This is a great starting point since you can go straight east of

the North Terrace highway to see most of the other cultural landmarks.
- Take the train. The train station is right in front of the Parliament building.

Cleland Conservation Park – the park includes three interesting destinations. All three are renowned for its natural beauty.

- **Cleland Wildlife Park** – some of the experiences that visitors can take part in at the park include night walks, getting up close with the koalas and other park animals, and so much more.
- **Mount Lofty summit** – this is the highest peak in the Mount Lofty mountain range. It's a favorite spot for locals and tourists alike because it provides an unequaled view of the city's skyline. It can also serve as a starting point for those who wish to visit the next item on this list: Waterfall Gully.
- **Waterfall Gully** – to be clear, Cleland Conservation Park encompasses 7 scenic waterfalls. Waterfall Gully is simply the largest and most picturesque among them.

Visitors who wish to see all the wondrous sights in the park may need to set aside at least two days on their itinerary. They may also want to bring some camping gear since there are several campsites scattered throughout the Park.

How to get there:
- Take the bus numbered 820S at stop E1 on the northern side of Currie Street. Alight at stop 19 on Greenhill Road. Walk a couple miles over to the southeast to reach Cleland Conservation Park.

- Take a car. There are several routes that you can follow by private car. It is best to bring a map of the area and ask around first prior to embarking on the trip. The drive should take around 55mins to 1 hour.

Adelaide Festival Centre – this structure is actually 3 months older than the Sydney Opera House. Although it is situated in the vicinity of the North Terrace Cultural Precinct, it is not considered part of the precinct. The building's architecture is a sight to behold, with three roofs that form distinct geometric patterns

The Festival Centre is home to the city's most celebrated festivals:
- The Adelaide Cabaret Festival
- The Adelaide International Guitar Festival (a biennial event)
- The Come Out Children's Festival

How to get there:
- Since the Festival Centre lies just meters away to the west from Government House, it would probably make sense to follow the same route that you'd take to get to North Terrace Cultural Precinct.

Adelaide Gaol – this is one of the oldest government-owned buildings in Adelaide (the other one being the Government House). It is the best place for tourists to go to if they want to have a spooky adventure. The gaol is said to be haunted by the spirits of the deceased. The most popular among these 'ghosts' is the gaol's first governor himself, William Baker Ashton.

Visitors can book Ghost Tours so that they can get a taste of what the gaol is like at night. Other tours offered include

Twilight Tours and History Tours. To get more information about the gaol or to book a tour, check out their website at http://adelaidegaol.org.au. Tourists can visit the gaol anytime during the daytime for unguided tours.

It opens Sundays to Saturdays at 9am and closes at 5pm though the final admission is only until 4pm.

How to get there:
- Note that there are no nearby bus stops to Adelaide Gaol. The best option is to take the J1A bus at Stop V2 on Currie Street. Disembark at Stop Y2, which is also on Currie Street although it is about 1.4 kilometers closer to the Gaol than Stop V2. From there, you'll have to walk to the Gaol.
- Take a car. This may require you to bring a map and ask around for the best routes to take. Just note that turning right onto Gaol Road is prohibited, so it is best to check for alternate routes.
- Hire a taxi. This is by far, the best and safest option.

Glenelg Beach – this is Adelaide's most historic beach because it is where the first settlement was established. The beach is part of a lovely seaside village that is also named Glenelg. This means that there's so much for tourists to do there aside from just swimming and sunbathing. History buffs can take walks along around to take photos of structures that have been around since the late 1800s. These include the Glenelg Jetty, the Stamford Grand or Pier Hotel, the Town Hall, and the beautiful gardens of the Partridge House.

How to get there:

- Take the tram at Victoria Square. Disembark at Stop 17 along Moseley Square, which is right at the heart of Glenelg.
- Take bus number 263 at Stop E1 on the eastern side of King William Street. Disembark at Stop 23 on Brighton Road. Walk from there towards Jetty Road until you reach your destination. Another option is to take bus H20 at Stop U2 on the south side of Grenfell Street. This should take you straight to Moseley Street at the Zone D stop. That means there'd be no need to walk to Glenelg from the Bus stop.

Penfolds Magill Estate - Penfolds Magill Estate is a popular winery to visit, not least because it is the home of Penfolds Grange, where the most expensive wine in Australia is created. In addition to the winery, however, the estate is home to a variety of other attractions to explore, especially if you are interested in Australian archaeology. Penfolds Magill Estate includes the winery, administration area, the barrel room, a tasting room (where all bottles ever produced are shown), as well as an elegant bistro, ideal for a spot of lunch and a glass of wine. You can even see the first cottage Dr. Penfold ever constructed, along with the first vines planted. The estate is a short 15 minute drive away from the center of the city, making it easily accessible, and there are two different tours visitors can choose from. If you want to try a private wine tasting session then please book ahead in advance.

How To Get There

- **Address**: 78 Penfold Road, Magill, 5072
- Take a bus from the city to Penfold Road

Seal Bay Conservation Park- Kangaroo Island is popular and once done, you may think that's all there is to experience, but the Seal Bay Conservation Park, which is situated on Kangaroo Island, is something truly spectacular. Visitors here actually have the opportunity to interact with a breeding colony of sea lions and learn about all the ways the park, and everyone else, can help support them in the wild. There's a boardwalk you can cross in order to enjoy fantastic views of the sea lions, but the tours are incredible. During the summer months, the park stays open until late, and watching these creatures at dusk is a truly awesome spectacle.

How To Get There
- **Address**: Seal Bay Road, Kangaroo Island, 5221
- There are no public buses to the Seal Conservation Park. Visitors are encouraged to drive.

A lot of travel experts agree that the best time to visit the city is on the months of February to March. This is when the annual Adelaide Festival of Arts is celebrated. This year, the festival is going to last from the 26th of February to the 14th of March. The Festival of Arts is a colorful celebration that encompasses all the artistic fields. A lot of the celebrations are also conducted at the North Terrace Cultural Precinct, though some events may also be conducted in parks and other establishments.

7.2 Where to Eat

Red Ochre and the River Café – these are two different restaurants on the same building. The lower level houses the River Café while the Red Ochre Grill is situated on the upper level. The Red Ochre Grill has an extensive wine list that includes authentic South Australian wines mixed in with classic Italian flavors. Since both establishments are owned and managed by the Rey Mauger and his team, they have the same website address: http://www.redochre.com.au.

You can also call +61 8 8211 8555 for inquiries and reservations.

Adelaide Casino – the Adelaide Casino building hosts a collection of restaurants that are run by world-class chefs. Most of the restaurants serve lunch, dinner, and snacks. Each restaurant in the Casino has its own special menu that ranges from authentic Asian cuisine, to a mixture of French-Vietnamese cuisine, to New York-style dining and so on.

Adelaide Casino is located right at the top of the North Terrace railway station. This means that you can go there directly for dinner and a few games of chips right after exploring the North Terrace Cultural Precinct.

Penfolds Magill Estate Restaurant – the restaurant is located near the historic Magill Estate Vineyard, which was founded in 1844. The restaurant itself is located in a historic building: Penfolds' spiritual home. The home has since been redeveloped into a modern architectural gem.

As expected, Penfolds Magill Estate Restaurant includes a list of the best and oldest wines in Australia. Its degustation menu includes a list of contemporary food with locally-sourced ingredients. But the food and the wine are not the only reasons why the restaurant is so popular. It also provides great views of the Mount Lofty foothills, which should make for some sigh-worthy Instagram selfies.

The restaurant is also located about 12 minutes away from the Cleland Conservation Park going through the road along Waterfall Gully. The drive there should take a scenic route since you'll also be passing through the Mount Osmond Reserve.

1877 Restaurant - This charming Italian restaurant is housed within a former school – the first restaurant in the city to do. Instead of teaching schoolchildren how to do their ABC's, guests are now having a lesson in how Italian cuisine should be experienced. 1877 Restaurant offers a delicious menu of traditional dishes, a great drinks menu and a cozy atmosphere, boasting several private dining rooms and even a roaring fireplace. The atmosphere is sophisticated and elegant, while still retaining a warm and friendly service, which makes it a wonderful place to dine.

7.3 Where to Stay

Intercontinental Adelaide – an award-winning 5-star hotel that is conveniently located in North Terrace. This is the best option for tourists who are visiting Adelaide to immerse in its rich cultural heritage. Reservations and inquiries can be made at http://www.icadelaide.com.au or by calling their toll free number at 1800 593 932.

Crafers Cottages – this is located in the hills near Cleland Conservation Park. This is a great starting point for tourists who wish to experience the outdoors through nature walks in the bushland, tours of vineyards and wineries, and so on. Guests are also housed in separate cottages, which means that they would have more privacy and they'd be able to bring the family dog too. For more information, check out http://www.craferscottages.com.au or call +61 (8) 8339 4151.

Stamford Grand Adelaide – this is the best option for tourists who wish to have a view of the sea from their hotel rooms. Located in Glenelg, the Stamford Grand is just a few meters from the Glenelg jetty and from the long stretch of Glenelg Beach. Reservations and inquiries can be made at http://www.stamford.com.au or by calling +61 (8) 8376 1222. You can also send an email to reservations@sga.stamford.com.au.

Thorngrove Manor Hotel - If you are searching for beauty, sophistication, privacy and enchantment, then look no further than Thorngrove Manor. So much more than a mere resort, it is an experience all by itself. Thorngrove Manor is a member of the Small Luxury Hotels of the World, boasting elegant and stylish private accommodation for prestigious guests. There is a sense of old world magic and charm in every detail but still featuring all the state of the art luxuries and technology. From the comfort of the private accommodation, guests can take in panoramic views of stunning grounds, before heading back inside where careful attention has been taken to ensure the comfort of guests. In addition to all of this, privacy is so important that guests may never actually see anyone else staying at the Manor. Address: 2 Glenside Lane, Stirling, South Australia 5152

7.4 Adelaide Nightlife

Adelaide has a wide selection of nightclubs and bars to choose from. But if you want a truly memorable experience, it is best to hit any of the pubs that are scattered around the city. There are at least 70 pubs in the CBD alone, most of which have been standing right where they are since the early years of the colony. Disregard the misconception that the sole purpose for going to a pub is to drink.

Most of the pubs in Adelaide today also offer other forms of entertainment including live music and dancing. For a more interesting experience, go to a pub that has a specific theme such as an Irish pub or a British pub. Most of the pubs are located in the same vicinity as the nightclubs and bars, so you shouldn't have any problem with hopping from one establishment to another.

Adelaide Casino - If you're searching for an energetic, pulsating entertainment venue but not a nightclub, then make your way to Adelaide Casino. The city's only casino venue, it is spread out over three floors within the old Railway Station in the center of Adelaide. Inside, the recent multi-million dollar renovation has transformed it into a world-class establishment. Stylish and sophisticated, it features bars, restaurants, cafes and gambling area. Visitors can try their luck at a wide range of games before heading to Madame Hanoi for a French-Vietnamese fusion meal or to the Oasis Outdoor Bar where you can enjoy a pizza or other dishes cooked in a traditional wood oven.

Address: North Terrace, Adelaide, South Australia 5000

Zhivago - Located in Adelaide's Central Business District, Zhivago stands out from all the other nightclubs in the area. Everything about this club screams "I am the best" and it's not hard to see why when you step inside. Zhivago relocated here from the Colonial Light Square in 2011 and has managed to maintain its somewhat grunge atmosphere for which it's always been known for.

Inside, the polished cement floors and the graffiti art really do set the scene, giving it a refreshing look compared to other nightclubs. Look down between the feet of those on the dance floor and you may even see splashes of paint on the floor, which then lights up underneath the disco lights.

Depending on what theme night you come on, the drinks specials do vary, but expect it to always be on spirit and a beer. However, there are a wide selection of other beers, spirits, wines and cocktails on offer, both imported and domestic. Friday and Saturday nights are always packed with those looking to kick off the weekends. During the week, the club is quieter, typically visited by those who have finished work.

The club has a great dance floor to enjoy and when you need to rest your feet for a bit, there are several couches you can rest on. The music is extremely loud and usually plays anything and everything from the 90s right until the top 40 today. Theme nights are put on every so often, but everything is something you can dance to.

Zhivago also boasts two recently introduced VIP areas where visitors can enjoy secured semi-private booths just a little away from the chaos of the dance floor. This is great if you're out with a group and are cordoned off by screens and curtains.

What makes Zhivago different from other nightclubs is that food is served. So when you need refreshments, you can have both the liquid and solid types.

Address: 54 Currie Street Basement, Adelaide.

Uni Bar - Australia isn't just for the rich and experienced; it's a great place for students and backpackers. For those who desperately need to wind down and take a break from their studies, the Uni Bar is the ideal place to go. Located on the fifth floor of the Union House on campus, Uni Bar is open to students and everyone else. It's opened primarily on weekdays, and is always packed with university students and the younger crowd looking for a great escape.

The Uni Bar regularly hosts smaller bands and acts from the local area as well as from other areas in Australia. It's also frequented by locals who want to enjoy the cheaper drinks, play a few games of pool and enjoy some conversation before heading off to the bigger clubs. The Uni Bar is also on the rounds of the Engineering Pub Crawl, where nearly a thousand people attend a pub crawl.

A lot of the action is centered around the pool tables, where guests get the chance to show off their skills. It also gives them a chance to get away from the loud music near the bar. The bar serves a variety of beers, spirits and soft drinks, all of which are the cheapest you'll find in the city. There are two Happy Hours each day, where the drinks are crazy cheap and the food is simple, tasty and, of course, on the cheaper side of things.

Address: Union Building, Kintore Av, Adelaide, SA

Jive - Located on the west side of Hindley Street, Jive is a relaxed and chilled out club, which often sees an influx of university students and the younger crowds. The club hosts various DJs, live bands and acts from all over Australia and the rest of the world. The cover fee varies depending on who is lined up for that night and once the acts have finished and left the building, there is a DJ ready to take things all through the night.

As soon as you get into the club, you'll notice a massive dance floor between the entryway, the bar and the stage. Most people will head for either the bar or the dance floor. While the club is always packed, and is on the larger side, there are still corners where the atmosphere is more cozy, and the whole ambience to it all is fun, friendly and relaxing. Everyone is welcomed here, and you will come across a wide variety of people.

The decor of the club is not quite as well presented as it was when it first opened, and each part of it is decked out in a different color, including one wall offering a fantastic satirical version of the city. The walls are also lined with brightly colored posters of bands who have played here. Some of the tables are actually barrels but the only real seating area is a few sofas which line the dance floor. They are quite in demand when you've danced so much your feet screams above the music to give them a much-needed rest. However, when their screams have dulled to a mere whisper, head back up to the dance floor and start the process all over again.

The drinks are plentiful and varied, offering everything from beers to wines, from cocktails to hard liquors. Prices are quite reasonable, especially compared to other clubs in the area.

Address: 181 Hindley St, Adelaide SA

Chapter 8: Cairns

Often referred to as the gateway to the tropical north, Cairns exudes an air of refinement and sophistication. Boasting stylish cities, world renowned attractions, a tropical climate and a relaxed atmosphere, Cairns is one of Australia's top destinations.

Wonders, both natural and manmade, await you here. The Great Barrier Reef and the Daintree Rainforest are just two of the stunning natural landscapes that wait for you to explore. Port Douglas and Mission Beach are great for those seeking relaxation. For those who enjoy cultural experiences, there's nothing better than enjoying a ride on the Kuranda railway or following the Great Tropical Drive where white water rivers and the Tablelands await.

Visitors can even try a taste of the outback via Cape Tribulation or the Savannah Way. Along with the Great Barrier Reef and the tropical rainforest, Cairns and the surrounding region are famous for their natural beauty.

For those seeking manmade beauty, Cairns is well-known for its charming cafes and restaurants where you can dine on locally sourced dishes before heading off to see what's available at the many outdoor markets. The laid back atmosphere and pleasant climate makes Cairns an ideal location for everyone, regardless of budget or age.

8.1 Where to Go – Best Places for Sightseeing and Adventure

The Great Barrier Reef - It is impossible to visit Cairns and not explore the wonders of the Great Barrier Reef. Famous as the world's biggest coral reef system, it consists of almost 3,000 separate reefs spread out over 344,400 square meters (or 133,000 square miles), and is actually visible from space! Visitors can jump onto any one of the numerous boats that take you out to sea, allowing you to dive and snorkel in and out of the wondrous reefs. You can stay for just a few hours but there are options, which allow you to stay out on a diving cruise stay.

Experience Aboriginal Culture - The Aborigines are Australia's indigenous ethnic group who have lived here for over 40,000 years. There's no better place to explore the rich history of the world's oldest living culture than at the Tjapukai Aboriginal Cultural Park. It's a short fifteen minute drive away from the city, but it's a fantastic place to explore. In addition to exhibitions and workshops, the cultural park also puts on live performances of story telling, dancing and music.

If you fancy delving deep into Aboriginal culture and history, head north to the Mossman Gorge Centre. Here, visitors can explore the beauty of the gorge and learn about the Kuku Yalanji culture.

Skyrail Rainforest Cableway and Kuranda Scenic Railway with Kuranda - Kuranda is a charming little village inundated with natural charms in the midst of a stunning tropical forest. Not only is it abound in beautiful landscapes, but it is renowned for its artistic community. Main street is lined with fig trees and it's not surprising to see parrots and butterflies flittering from tree to flower along the way. The village boasts a number of art galleries, markets and stores in which visitors can browse before heading to the top attraction here.

The Skyrail Rainforest Cable car takes you on a magical ride over the rainforest for an hour and half. Visitors can get off at the Red Peak and the Barron Falls Stations so you can explore before carrying on with your journey.

The Kuranda Scenic Railway is the ideal experience when you're ready to return to Cairns. Over a period of two hours, visitors can journey through some of the most beautiful scenery on a railway, which has been making this route for over a hundred years.

Market Shopping - The Esplanade Market held on Saturdays are a great way to experience Cairns. Here, visitors can purchase a wide range of goods from clothing to jewelry, from sweet treats to handmade beauty products that even the stars use.

For night markets, there's no better place to head to than the night market at Palm Cove. It's always held on a Friday night and everything is available here.

Rusty's is the market to visit when you fancy purchasing the best fresh foods. It's all available here – from pineapples to nuts.

The Holloway Beach Markets is great if you want to experience a great friendly atmosphere and even better food.

The Daintree Rainforest - Said to be the oldest rainforest in the world, Daintree is the Must See attraction when visiting Cairns. Dating back to 135 million years ago, Daintree Rainforest is a World Heritage Site situated around two hours north of the city center. Located within the thick tangles of the trees, are the world's largest range of animals. The spring period is when you see them more, when the temperatures have dropped a little but the rainy season hasn't started. At dawn, you can hear the birds sing before heading to the beaches for a quick dip.

The Daintree Rainforest is easily accessible from Cairns as well as Port Douglas and Cape Tribulation. To get the full experience, why not opt to stay in one of the eco lodges that have been established within the rainforest itself or stay with Daintree Village along the river. The best way to take in all the outstanding beauty is through the aerial walkways or along the numerous trails marked out for hikers. Butterflies of all colors and shapes flit to and fro, while the endangered cassowary peeks through the trees – will you be able to spot its vibrant blue neck? Don't forget to see the famous zamia fern that is over 600 million years old! It features a trunk, which has grown underground in order to protect itself against the dinosaurs before they were wiped out.

A true experience of Daintree Rainforest wouldn't be complete without a cruise down the river. From the safety of the boat you can look out for crocodiles that swim freely here, along with the turtles.

Fact: Around two thirds of the country's bat and butterfly species can be found living within the Daintree Rainforest in addition to a third of Australia's reptile and frog species.

In addition to the various butterflies, bats, frogs, reptiles and marsupials that live here, the rainforest is home to nearly 430 bird species, which includes thirteen species which are native to this area alone. Listening to the sounds of all these birds is mesmerizing when the sun peeks across the horizon and captivating as you cruise along the river. If you come here during the spring, you may find it deafening. This is because it's breeding season and they are defending their territory or trying to entice a mate. Some of the birds that can be found within the branches of the rainforest include cuckoos, kingfishers, nightjars, the spotted catbirds and wompoo fruit dove.

When you need to relax after hours of trekking through the wondrous rainforest, Daintree boasts a number of idyllic beaches with soft sands perfect for lying on and surrounded by crystal clear waters. Most of them can be found near Cape Tribulation where the rainforest encounters the ocean. In fact, this is the sole place where two World Heritage Sites comes together. The most popular beach is Coconut Beach, but Donovan's Beach and Noah's Beach are just as pretty.

Hartleys Creek Crocodile Adventure Park - If visiting Cairns with kids – or even if it's just by yourself – pay a visit to Hartley's Creek Crocodile Adventure Park. There are a multitude of crocodiles that live here, but the park also features a variety of other creatures that live here. There are several habitats to explore, each with a range of native wildlife to the Queensland region, including the endangered cassowary. Visitors can watch crocodiles sunbathe on the banks before listening to several wildlife talks, and take in a snake or crocodile show. Don't forget to feed a koala yourself and the boat cruise over Harleys Lagoon is a must.

8.2 Where to Eat

There's a wide selection of restaurants and cafes to choose from when visiting the city. Whether you fancy dining al fresco or within the grandeur of a five star establishment, there's something for everyone.

Dundee's Restaurant On The Waterfront - To make a great restaurant experience you need three things – exceptional food, perfect location, and the ideal atmosphere. Dundee's Restaurant On The Waterfront blends all three, creating the perfect package. Situated right on the boardwalk, diners can gaze out over the Marlin Marina and the Trinity Inlet with the mountains to the side. Open every day for lunch and dinner, it offers a range of culinary delights in order to suit all palates with the views offering the perfect backdrop.

Address: 1 Marlin Parade, (Shop 3), Cairns, Queensland 4870

Ochre Restaurant and Catering - The Ochre Restaurant and Catering is one of the most famous restaurants throughout the country. It was known previously as the Red Ochre Grill with a reputation for serving innovative Australian dishes using locally sourced organic ingredients. Out of all the restaurants in the city, the Ochre Restaurant is the number one dining establishment to visit.

Address: 43 Shields Street, Cairns, Queensland 4870

8.3 Where to Stay

Vision Cairns Esplanade - If you are searching for a room with a view then there is no better place to stay than at Vision Cairns Esplanade. This luxury hotel boasts exquisite vistas of the Coral Sea from many rooms and facilities. Vision Cairns Esplanade is a recent addition to the city's smorgasbord of premier accommodation with great management and staff ready to make your stay enjoyable.

There is a variety of accommodation to choose from, include self-contained sea and mountain view rooms, a penthouse suite and poolside apartments. The hotel features charming gardens, two swimming pools, a fully equipped gym, a spa, steam room and BBQ area.

Vision Cairns Esplanade is ideally located, close to the marina, and surrounded by a range of restaurants, cafes, bars, galleries and boutiques.

Address: 125 - 129 Esplanade, Cairns, Queensland 4870.

Water's Edge Apartments Cairns - The Water's Edge Apartments Cairns is situated along the Cairns Esplanade with stunning vistas over the Esplanade and the Trinity Inlet. These luxury apartments are ideal for visitors who prefer the finer things in life, but still within a reasonable price bracket and retaining a dream home experience.

At the Water's Edge Apartments Cairns, guests can relax in comfortable surroundings, with each apartment styled differently to each other. All apartments feature a kitchen, living and dining area and light, airy bedrooms with en suite bathrooms. From the comfort of the oversized balconies, guests can enjoy panoramic views over the sea whereas guests staying on the ground floor have swim out decks.

From the Water's Edge Apartments Cairns, guests only have a short walk before being surrounded by a variety of restaurants, bars, shops and other entertainment venues.

Address: 155 The Esplanade, Cairns, Queensland 4870

Cairns Coconut Holiday Resort - The Cairns Coconut Holiday Resort is located around seven kilometers south of the city and is a recent winner of the prestigious Australian and Queensland Tourism Award. The resort is set within 28 acres of tropical gardens and boasts a wide variety of amenities and facilities designed to make your stay here memorable for all the right reasons. Guests can learn more about these facilities in the Nemo Buggy.

Some of the facilities to enjoy here include the Mini Coconuts Playground, designed for the entertainment of younger guests, as well as the Play Hub, the Splash Waterpark, the gigantic jumping pillows and playground. While the kids are sorted, parents can enjoy the garden pool where water aerobics and other classes are held, otherwise enjoy the bar or the family movies on the outdoor screen. A supermarket, launderette, gym and Wi-Fi are just a few of the other amenities at the Cairns Coconut Holiday Resort.

Variety is key at the resort. As such, there's a range of accommodation to choose from – self-contained villas, cabins, and condos – all ranging in price and size. There is even sites for caravans and campers to use if you don't want to give up the wheels.

Address: 23 -5 1 Anderson Road, Woree, Cairns, Queensland 4868

8.4 Cairns Nightlife

The majority of Cairns' nightlife can be found along Spence Street, also known as the Strip. Running along the side of the Esplanade on the southern section, there are a wide range of bars, clubs and entertainment venues to choose from. It's popular with locals and those passing through while staying on a budget, and as such the atmosphere can seem a little untamed compared to other sections of the city. The best thing is that with so many options here, there's something to suit every taste.

Gilligan's Nightclub - In 2013, Gilligan's Nightclub was declared the Number One Nightclub in Cairns and it's not hard to see why. It is one of the biggest clubs in the city, frequented by locals and visitors, who want nothing more than to drink until dawn and get down and boogie on the wooden deck dance floor. Open seven nights a week, it also features a poolside and al fresco sections when you need some fresh air. The club is spread out over three different sections, boasting air conditioning, large screen TVs, a lagoon pool with a manmade sand beach and grass area. The bar upstairs offers a wide variety of drinks, from beers to cocktails, as well as heart-racing live music and DJs to take you into the wee hours.

Address: 57 - 89 Grafton St, Cairns, Queensland 4870.

The Woolshed Char Grill and Saloon Bar - Located on Spence Street, the Woolshed Char Grill and Saloon Bar – or just simply, the Woolshed – is an iconic part of the city and is famous amongst travellers as one of the cheapest places in Cairns to drink and eat and for patrons climbing onto the tables to dance.

The Woolshed has been open to the public for nearly 20 years and continues to enjoy success as one of the greatest bars in the city. It won the award for Queensland's Best Backpacker Venue for four years and is renowned for its extremely loud music.

Address: 24 Shields Street, City Place, Cairns, Queensland 4870

The Pier Bar and Grill - If you're searching for fun, vibrancy but with style, then head to the Pier Bar and Grill. This club is located within the Pier complex with fantastic views across the Cairns Esplanade and the Coral Sea. It's a popular place with both locals and visitors to the city, with a somewhat exotic atmosphere. Spread out over different levels, the indoor section includes a comfortable and relaxing seating area with tables and lounges, pool tables and a dance floor where you can get your groove on. The outside area includes a decking area where you can get a breath of fresh air whilst gazing out over the water.

Address: 1 Pierpoint Road, The Pier Shopping Centre, Cairns, Queensland 4870

The Union Jack Hotel - The Union Jack Hotel, or just The Jack to locals, is one of those pubs you just keep coming back to. In 2013, it was voted as the best pub in the city. Since it was first opened, it has changed names several times as well as expanding its facilities. The Jack is more than simple a pub – it features a hotel, hostel for backpackers, a restaurant, gaming area, entertainment venue and so much more.

If you are searching for a great atmosphere in which to socialize in, then The Jack is the ideal place to visit. It boasts an indoor and outdoor entertainment area, two indoor bars that serve an array of tasty beverages, and even features a variety of bands from all over Australia. On Saturday nights, the Jack turns into a club and everyone rocks until the sun comes up.

Address: Cnr Spence & Sheridan Sts, Cairns, Queensland 4870

The Heritage Bar-Pub-Club - You can find the Heritage Bar within a historic and listed building on the corner of Spence and Lake Streets, and is a fantastic amalgamation of nightclub and cozy pub. It's a popular hangout for locals and international visitors who are searching for a night of fun and partying. You can dance until your feet scream on one of the several dance floors or else you can socialize on the outdoor balconies where the couches are almost as relaxing as the views across the Central Business District.

The Heritage Bar – named after for the historic building it's house in – features a terrace bar, the outdoor balcony area, the club room where the DJ booth sits, dance floors and booths. Expect the music to be wickedly loud with numerous live bands playing on a regular basis, and expect to have a blast, Cairns style!

Address: Cnr Spence & Lake Street Cairns, Queensland 4870.

Chapter 9 - Australia Survival Guide (Safety!)

The secret to a truly memorable trip is to always be mindful of your safety. Despite the fact that Australia ranks high in terms of low crime rate and tourist safety, it would still be beneficial for tourists to always keep the following tips in mind:

- Avoid areas that have had some bad reputation in the past. Although most of these areas have already been rehabilitated in some way, there may still be some danger lurking about. One example of this is Kings Cross in Sydney. The area is still getting some mixed reviews although it is now a lot safer than it used to be in the 1990s. Some of the negative reviews state that Kings Cross is a haven for drug addicts, prostitutes, and other bad city elements.

- Watch out for deadly insects. These insects are actually more numerous than human criminals in Sydney. But there's no need to worry too much since two of the deadliest Aussie spiders are mostly found under rocks and overturned logs. That means there's no danger if you're staying in a hotel. The best way to avoid a spider bite when camping is to check every nook and cranny of the tent to make sure there are no unwanted guests.

Aside from insects, there are several other native Australian animals that may pose risks to your well-being. So always wear protective footwear when hiking in the hills and trails and heed the tour guide's warnings.

- Wear cool and comfortable clothing (in Sydney, men can even go around wearing nothing but shorts and flip-flops). The sun's heat is felt more intensely in Australia as compared to Europe or North America. To avoid sun exhaustion or heat stroke, it is best to wear comfortable summer clothing. Sometimes, even the winter days can also be hot. Also, don't forget to apply some sunscreen before heading out.

- Always heed the flags when swimming in the sea in any beach throughout Australia. The best way to stay safe is by staying the waters between the red and yellow flags. Night swimming is a no-no especially if you're alone or if the entire group has had one too many drinks.

Swimming outside of the flags puts you at risk for two possible dangers: falling victim to a shark attack or being carried away by strong currents or rips. Shark attacks don't normally happen in Australia's waters, but when it does, the results are often fatal.

- Write down the emergency hotline numbers for the city that you're currently in on a piece of paper and slip that onto a pocket of your every-day bag or wallet. The emergency number for ambulance, fire, and police assistance is the same for all states: 000.

Other emergency numbers that you have to keep track of include:

- Poisons Information Centre – 13 11 26

- Public Health Units – 1300 066 055

- Life line – 131 114

- Maritime and Aviation Rescue service – 9674 3000

- Police link – 131 444

- State Emergency Services (SES) (for assistance if you're trapped in a natural disaster or a bushfire) – 13 25 00

One final tip: don't forget to bring copies of your travel documents and identification cards everywhere. Keep the original copies somewhere safe.

Conclusion

Once again thank you for choosing *Lost Travelers*!

I hope we were able to provide you with the best travel tips when visiting Australia.

And we hope you enjoy your travels.

> *"Travel Brings Power and Love Back to Your Life"*
>
> - Rumi

Finally, if you enjoyed this book, then I'd like to ask you for a favor, would you be kind enough to leave a review for this book on Amazon? It'd be greatly appreciated!

- Simply search the keywords "Australia Travel Guide" on Amazon or go to our Author page "Lost Travelers" to review.

Please know that your satisfaction is important to us. If you were not happy with the book, please email us with the reason so we may serve you more accordingly next time.

- Email: Info@losttravelers.com

Thank you and good luck!

NOTES

NOTES

NOTES

NOTES

Preview Of 'New Zealand: The Ultimate New Zealand Travel Guide By A Traveler For A Traveler

Located 2,012 km to the south of Australia is New Zealand. There are two main islands comprising it, the North and South islands, and outlying islands scattered within the vicinity. Its two main islands are separated by a body of water known as the Cook Strait. The North Island is 829 km long. Its southern end is volcanic and because of this, there are plenty of excellent hot springs and geysers in the area. On the South island, lies the Southern Alps by the west end. Here is where one will find the highest point in New Zealand which is Mount Cook. It is 12,316 feet tall!

Some of the outlying islands are inhabited while others are not. The inhabited islands include Chatham, Great Barrier, and Stewart islands. The largest of the uninhabited islands are Campbell, Kermadec, Antipodes, and Auckland islands.

The first inhabitants of New Zealand were the Maoris. Their initial population was only 1,000 people. According to their oral history, it took the initial Maori population seven canoes to reach New Zealand from other parts of Polynesia. It was in the mid-1600s that the island cluster was explored by a man named Abel Tasma, a Dutch navigator. Another foreigner, a British by the name of James Cook, engaged in three voyages to New Zealand the first one taking place in 1769. New Zealand became a formal annex to Britain during the mid 1800s.

During this time, the Treaty of Waitangi was signed between Britain and the Maoris. It stated that there will be ample protection for Maori land should the Maoris accept British rule. Despite the treaty, tension between both factions intensified over time due to the continuous encroachment by British settlers.

Check out the rest of New Zealand: The Ultimate New Zealand Travel Guide on Amazon by simply searching it.

Check Out Our Other Guides

Below you'll find some of our other popular books that are on Amazon and Kindle as well. Simply search the titles below to check them out. Alternatively, you can visit our author page (Lost Travelers) on Amazon to see other work done by us.

- Vienna: The Ultimate Vienna Travel Guide By A Traveler For A Traveler

- Barcelona: The Ultimate Barcelona Travel Guide By A Traveler For A Traveler

- London: The Ultimate London Travel Guide By A Traveler For A Traveler

- Istanbul: The Ultimate Istanbul Travel Guide By A Traveler For A Traveler

- Vietnam: The Ultimate Vietnam Travel Guide By A Traveler For A Traveler

- Peru: The Ultimate Peru Travel Guide By A Traveler For A Traveler

- Australia: The Ultimate Australia Guide By A Traveler For A Traveler

- New Zealand: The Ultimate New Zealand Travel Guide By A Traveler For A Traveler

- Dublin: The Ultimate Dublin Travel Guide By A Traveler For A Traveler

- Thailand: The Ultimate Thailand Travel Guide By A Traveler For A Traveler

- Iceland: The Ultimate Iceland Travel Guide By A Traveler For A Traveler

- Santorini: The Ultimate Santorini Travel Guide By A Traveler For A Traveler

- Italy: The Ultimate Italy Travel Guide By A Traveler For A Traveler

You can simply search for these titles on the Amazon website to find them.

Made in the USA
Lexington, KY
23 February 2017